W9-BLK-433

You Know You're a
REPUBLICAN
★ ★ ★ ★ ★ ★
DEMOCRAT
If...

Frank Benjamin

 sourcebooks

Copyright © 2004, 2010 by Frank Benjamin
Cover and internal design © 2010 by Sourcebooks, Inc.
Cover design by Kristi Learoyd
Cover images © tharrison/iStockphoto.com

Sourcebooks and the colophon are registered trademarks of Sourcebooks, Inc.

All rights reserved. No part of this book may be reproduced in any form or by any electronic or mechanical means including information storage and retrieval systems—except in the case of brief quotations embodied in critical articles or reviews—without permission in writing from its publisher, Sourcebooks, Inc.

All brand names and product names used in this book are trademarks, registered trademarks, or trade names of their respective holders. Sourcebooks, Inc., is not associated with any product or vendor in this book.

Published by Sourcebooks, Inc.
P.O. Box 4410, Naperville, Illinois 60567-4410
(630) 961-3900
Fax: (630) 961-2168
www.sourcebooks.com

Library of Congress Cataloging-in-Publication Data

Benjamin, Frank.
  You know you're a Republican/Democrat if— / Frank Benjamin. — 2nd ed.
    p. cm.
  1. Republican Party (U.S. : 1854-)—Humor. 2. Democratic Party (U.S. : 1854-)—Humor. I. Title.
  PN6231.P6B39 2010
  818'.602—dc22
                                2010021502

Printed and bound in the United States of America.
VP 10 9 8 7 6 5 4 3 2 1

You Know You're a
REPUBLICAN If...

You're really looking forward to
Sarah Palin running for president.

You Know You're a
DEMOCRAT If...

You're really, *really* looking forward
to Sarah Palin running for president.

You Know You're a
REPUBLICAN If...

The far left leaning of President Obama is making you look forward to the next election because it will help Republicans win back congressional seats.

You Know You're a
DEMOCRAT If...

You didn't notice that President Obama has a far left leaning.

You Know You're a
REPUBLICAN If...

You start off on third base and
think you've hit a triple.

You Know You're a
DEMOCRAT If...

You hit a single but believe
you deserve a triple because
the other team got one.

You Know You're a
REPUBLICAN If...

You can't stand your gay uncle,
but you invite him to your son's
wedding because he's rich.

You Know You're a
DEMOCRAT If...

You can't stand your rich uncle, but
you invite him to your daughter's
graduation party because he's gay.

You Know You're a
REPUBLICAN If...

You've accepted that global warming
is real and that the polar ice caps
are melting at an alarming rate,
but you don't believe we should
panic and recklessly raise taxes
to fix it. You have, however,
invested in future beachfront
property—twenty miles inland.

You Know You're a
DEMOCRAT If...

For a long time now you've known
that: The sky is falling! The sky
is falling! No, wait. The sky is
cooking! The sky is cooking!

You Know You're a
REPUBLICAN If...

You can't fathom that Abraham
Lincoln was actually a Republican!

You Know You're a
DEMOCRAT If...

You can't fathom that Abraham
Lincoln was actually a Republican!

You Know You're a
REPUBLICAN If...

You're quietly disappointed that
the Iraq War turned into such a
quagmire, but you're sure we'll get
it right when we invade Iran.

You Know You're a
DEMOCRAT If...

You're strongly opposed to any military intervention in the sovereign affairs of other countries, unless Obama tells you it's the right thing to do.

You Know You're a
REPUBLICAN If...

You think public education is
broken and doesn't deserve more
money, and you send your children
to an expensive private school.

You Know You're a
DEMOCRAT If...

You think public education is
the backbone of America, but
it just needs more money, and
you send your children to an
expensive private school.

You Know You're a
REPUBLICAN If...

You believe the U.S. Constitution
clearly supports strip mining.

You Know You're a
DEMOCRAT If...

You believe the U.S. Constitution
clearly supports strippers.

You Know You're a
REPUBLICAN If...

You're very proud of your housekeeper's son who is serving in the U.S. military.

You Know You're a
DEMOCRAT If...

You don't personally know anyone
who is serving in the U.S. military.

You Know You're a
REPUBLICAN If...

You philosophically oppose
government welfare plans,
but you cash your Social
Security checks religiously.

You Know You're a
DEMOCRAT If...

You're philosophically appalled
by corporate America's emphasis
on profits, but you sure were
ticked off when your retirement
investments tanked.

You Know You're a
REPUBLICAN If...

There are three people in your household and you own four vehicles—not counting the ATVs.

You Know You're a
DEMOCRAT If...

The three cars you and your wife
own all get good gas mileage.

You Know You're a
REPUBLICAN If...

You think the only honorable
revolution in the history of mankind
was the American Revolution.

You Know You're a
DEMOCRAT If...

You think the only good
revolution is the one you're
personally going to lead.

You Know You're a
REPUBLICAN If...

You own a thirty-foot bullet speedboat named *Just Desserts*.

You Know You're a
DEMOCRAT If...

You own a thirty-foot sailboat
named *Guilty Pleasure*.

You Know You're a
REPUBLICAN If...

You're dealt a great hand at poker, you win big and gloat obnoxiously, but then you agree to buy the beer at the next game.

You Know You're a
DEMOCRAT If...

You beat your tennis partner
soundly two games in a row, feel
guilty, call it luck, and suggest
you play three out of five.

You Know You're a
REPUBLICAN If...

You support an increase in the U.S. military budget, especially for the base in your congressional district.

You Know You're a
DEMOCRAT If...

You want to slash the U.S. military budget, as long as they don't touch the base in your congressional district.

You Know You're a
REPUBLICAN If...

You blame overzealous home buyers for taking out unaffordable mortgages to buy oversized homes, which led to the bursting of the housing bubble. Now you're ticked off that your home is worth 20 percent less and you're anxious for the housing market to fix itself.

You Know You're a
DEMOCRAT If...

You blame overzealous mortgage
lenders and realtors for talking you
into a crazy mortgage for a big home
you really couldn't afford because
they said it was sure to go up 20
percent and you could refinance.
And you want the government to
fix them. Otherwise, you'd have
to take some blame yourself.

You Know You're a
REPUBLICAN If...

You've thought about becoming a
Libertarian, but you have trouble
with their philosophical support
of prostitution, gay marriage, and
uninhibited personal freedom.

You Know You're a
DEMOCRAT If...

You've thought about becoming a
Libertarian, but you have trouble
with their support of free trade.

You Know You're a
REPUBLICAN If...

You want to stem the tide of
illegal immigrants getting into
the United States. But then again,
somebody's got to mow your lawn.

You Know You're a
DEMOCRAT If...

You sort of sympathize with
undocumented workers ("illegal
immigrant" sounds so, well,
harsh), but the unions want the
borders closed and…Oh, shoot,
you're just so confused!

You Know You're a
REPUBLICAN If...

Your high school class voted
you Most Likely to Wear
Pinstripes or Prison Stripes.

You Know You're a
DEMOCRAT If...

Your high school class voted you
Most Likely to Change Gender.

You Know You're a
REPUBLICAN If...

Your vanity license plate reads: IMB4U.

You Know You're a
DEMOCRAT If...

Your vanity license plate
reads: LUVGOV.

You Know You're a
REPUBLICAN If...

When your son's soccer team came
in dead last at the tournament
but every player still got a trophy
just for "showing up," you sneered
and tossed the trophy in the
trash, and your son cried.

You Know You're a
DEMOCRAT If...

When your son's soccer team
won the tournament and every
player got a trophy saying "First
Place," you felt guilty and hid the
trophy, and your son cried.

You Know You're a
REPUBLICAN If...

You have a tender spot in your heart for corporate tax attorneys.

You Know You're a
DEMOCRAT If...

You have a tender spot in your heart
for product liability trial lawyers.

You Know You're a
REPUBLICAN If...

You prefer your steaks rare, your jokes
raw, and Democrats "skewered."

You Know You're a
DEMOCRAT If...

You prefer your vegetables raw,
you don't eat meat, and you don't
tell jokes because jokes are about
victimhood and you don't want
to have any part in that—unless
the jokes are about Republicans.

You Know You're a
REPUBLICAN If...

You favor free speech, except
for burning the flag or criticizing
U.S. military policy.

You Know You're a
DEMOCRAT If...

You favor free speech, except for ugly
words about minorities, the disabled,
or endangered species. Or you.

You Know You're a
REPUBLICAN If...

You're a political history buff and you're convinced John F. Kennedy "stole" the 1960 presidential election because of vote tampering by Chicago's Mayor Daley.

You Know You're a
DEMOCRAT If...

You're a political history buff and you think George W. Bush "stole" the 2000 presidential election because of vote tampering by the U.S. Supreme Court.

You Know You're a
REPUBLICAN If...

Sure, you'd really like to be concerned about the little guy, but you're terrified the government will tax the rich more and stifle economic growth.

You Know You're a
DEMOCRAT If...

You don't worry much about economic growth as long as we tax the rich more.

You Know You're a
REPUBLICAN If...

You'd give up your marriage and the governorship of South Carolina to be with your "soul mate" in Argentina.

You Know You're a
DEMOCRAT If...

You didn't know
Republicans had souls.

You Know You're a
REPUBLICAN If...

You ran for county dogcatcher on a platform of smaller government, lower taxes, respect for the flag, and withdrawing from the UN.

You Know You're a
DEMOCRAT If...

You ran for county dogcatcher so
you could let the dogs go free.

You Know You're a
REPUBLICAN If...

When you were teaching your son
to ride a bike, you made him wear
a helmet, and when he fell off, you
told him to get right back on.

You Know You're a
DEMOCRAT If...

You bought your son a bike helmet too, but before you let him on a bike you made sure your union health insurance benefits covered injuries from bike accidents, and, just for backup, you researched to see if anyone had successfully sued Schwinn when their kids got hurt.

You Know You're a
REPUBLICAN If...

You've watched the war movie
The Dirty Dozen six times, and
every time you cried at the end.

You Know You're a
DEMOCRAT If...

You cried watching *Bambi* as a kid, and
you've been in therapy ever since.

You Know You're a
REPUBLICAN If...

You prove your racial sensitivity by saying *gracias* to your gardener.

You Know You're a
DEMOCRAT If...

You're strongly committed to racial equality even if you don't personally have any friends of a different race.

You Know You're a
REPUBLICAN If...

You shop at Whole Foods natural
grocery stores because you don't
mind paying a little extra for good
quality food. But you'd prefer it
if the checkout person combed
his hair and wore deodorant.

You Know You're a
DEMOCRAT If...

You absolutely must buy your
groceries at Whole Foods even if
your rent money goes toward organic
apples, heirloom tomatoes, and
all-natural, hormone-free yogurt.
You *are* the checkout person.

You Know You're a
REPUBLICAN If...

You blame the Democrats for the regulations that prohibit you from enjoying toasty fires in your beloved wood-burning fireplace. So you go ahead and burn them anyway.

You Know You're a
DEMOCRAT If...

You blame the Republicans for the lack of industrial pollution controls that led to the rules restricting fires in your beloved wood-burning stove. So you go ahead and burn them anyway.

You Know You're a
REPUBLICAN If...

You proudly shop at Wal-Mart.

You Know You're a
DEMOCRAT If...

Because of Wal-Mart's terrible
reputation for low-wage labor, sexism,
and manufacturing its products
at overseas sweatshops, you only
shop at Wal-Mart late at night
when no one will recognize you.

You Know You're a
REPUBLICAN If...

You have a picture of yourself
shaking hands with Ronald Reagan
hanging on your office wall.

You Know You're a
DEMOCRAT If...

You have a picture of Ronald
Reagan hanging in the middle
of your dart board.

You Know You're a
REPUBLICAN If...

Someone calling you an "intellectual" would make you very uncomfortable because you just know that's a code word for "Commie" or, worse, "Democrat."

You Know You're a
DEMOCRAT If...

Someone calling you "anti-intellectual" would make you uncomfortable because that's your code word for "Republican."

You Know You're a
REPUBLICAN If...

You stand behind the constitutional
right of lobbyists to "petition the
government," so you gladly take
their campaign contributions.

You Know You're a
DEMOCRAT If...

You're not at all comfortable
with the powerful influence of
lobbyists, so you *quietly* take
their campaign contributions.

You Know You're a
REPUBLICAN If...

You think Sarah Palin is the second coming of Ronald Reagan, but a little prettier.

You Know You're a
DEMOCRAT If...

You think Sarah Palin is the
second coming of Dan Quayle, but
without his masterful intellect.

You Know You're a
REPUBLICAN If...

You've conveniently forgotten
that the Environmental Protection
Agency was created during
the Nixon administration.

You Know You're a
DEMOCRAT If...

You still don't believe the
EPA was created during the
Nixon administration.

You Know You're a
REPUBLICAN If...

You wish Chinese food didn't
have so much MSG in it.

You Know You're a
DEMOCRAT If...

You think the MSG in Chinese food
should be regulated by the FDA,
the Department of Agriculture, the
Center for Disease Control, the FBI,
the Defense Department, and Oprah.

You Know You're a
REPUBLICAN If...

You were quite upset that Tiger Woods failed to live up to his sacred wedding vows. But you're not surprised given that he's a godless Buddhist anyway. He's probably a Democrat too! You wouldn't, however, turn down a chance to play a round of golf with him.

You Know You're a
DEMOCRAT If...

You were saddened that Tiger Woods
turned out to be another athletic hero
who couldn't keep his pants zipped.
But he's probably just a hypocritical
rich Republican anyway. You wouldn't,
however, turn down a chance to
play a round of golf with him.

You Know You're a
REPUBLICAN If...

You're convinced that, no matter what, it's important to keep Iran's nuclear ambitions in check.

You Know You're a
DEMOCRAT If...

You wonder if Iran would
behave better if we'd just
send them a big check.

You Know You're a
REPUBLICAN If...

Someone calling you a
"liberal" makes you mad.

You Know You're a
DEMOCRAT If...

Someone calling you a "liberal"
makes you squirm.

You Know You're a
REPUBLICAN If...

Someone calling you a "conservative"
makes you feel patriotic.

You Know You're a
DEMOCRAT If...

Someone calling you a "patriot"
makes you worry they think
you're conservative.

You Know You're a
REPUBLICAN If...

At one time you were an exotic
pole dancer, but you saw the error
of your ways, found God, started
wearing stylish but modest clothing,
developed a taste for Tiffany jewelry,
and joined the Junior League—after
you became pregnant by and married
one of your rich customers.

You Know You're a
DEMOCRAT If...

You are a pole dancer.

You Know You're a
REPUBLICAN If...

You don't like your mother-in-law,
but you act nice to her because your
wife is first in line for the inheritance.

You Know You're a
DEMOCRAT If...

You can't stand your mother-in-law, but you act nice to her because it's the right thing to do and you're living in her house.

You Know You're a
REPUBLICAN If...

You thought the rallying cry "Save
the icebergs!" was referring to
your favorite type of lettuce.

You Know You're a
DEMOCRAT If...

For your vacation you traveled via trawler to the Arctic to observe firsthand the melting ice caps. Plus, you would never be caught dead eating iceberg lettuce. (Arugula, anyone?)

You Know You're a
REPUBLICAN If...

You hate President Obama,
but not because he's black.

You Know You're a
DEMOCRAT If...

You love President Obama,
but not because he's black.

You Know You're a
REPUBLICAN If...

When you play Scrabble, the word
D-E-M-O-C-R-A-T is not allowed.

You Know You're a
DEMOCRAT If...

When you play Scrabble, the word "Republican" is spelled L-O-S-E-R.

You Know You're a
REPUBLICAN If...

You were appalled when a mob of
enviro-wackos threw tomatoes at
your rally *against* the Copenhagen
global warming agreement.

You Know You're a
DEMOCRAT If...

You were appalled that the
tomatoes weren't organic.

You Know You're a
REPUBLICAN If...

When your daughter failed to make the soccer "A" team, you got her a trainer and told her to work harder.

You Know You're a
DEMOCRAT If...

When your daughter failed
to make the soccer "A" team,
you got her a cello.

You Know You're a
REPUBLICAN If...

You think more criminals should
be locked up for as long as possible,
and new jails to hold them could be
built with money made by selling
advertising on school buses...or selling
the Grand Canyon to the Chinese...
or cutting back on food stamps...
or something like that surely!

You Know You're a
DEMOCRAT If...

You think criminals had rough childhoods and could use a little TLC.

You Know You're a
REPUBLICAN If...

You've never seen a government social services program that you thought justified raising your taxes.

You Know You're a
DEMOCRAT If...

You've never seen a social services program that you weren't willing to spend other taxpayers' money on.

You Know You're a
REPUBLICAN If...

You have a home aquarium. The big fish kills the little fish. So you get another big fish. They fight constantly. "Animals are like that," you think.

You Know You're a
DEMOCRAT If...

You own a home aquarium. The big
fish kills the little fish. You hold a
funeral for the little fish. You are
at a loss for what to do. You give
away the big fish. You put the empty
aquarium in the attic. "Whew,
no more fighting," you think.

You Know You're a
REPUBLICAN If...

When you were a teenager, you
worked after school to save money.
You bought a used Ford pickup.
Your friend's dad bought her a
new Mustang. You were envious.
You wanted to swap dads.

You Know You're a
DEMOCRAT If...

Your dad bought you a cute new Mustang. You felt guilty. You felt guilty every day. You did nothing.

You Know You're a
REPUBLICAN If...

You think government agencies should be run like businesses, with management free to fire incompetent employees at will.

You Know You're a
DEMOCRAT If...

You think businesses should be
run like government agencies,
with workers protected from firing
no matter how incompetent.

You Know You're a
REPUBLICAN If...

At some point in your life you won a skeet shooting trophy, a polo playing trophy, or a trophy wife.

You Know You're a
DEMOCRAT If...

You received the Good Conduct
Award in grade school.

You Know You're a
REPUBLICAN If...

You don't pray much yourself,
but you zealously defend the
idea of prayer in schools.

You Know You're a
DEMOCRAT If...

You insist upon a strict separation
of church and state, unless it
threatens your daughter's federal
financial aid to Notre Dame.

You Know You're a
REPUBLICAN If...

You spend considerable amounts of
your time and money on causes you're
devoted to—like gun ownership.

You Know You're a
DEMOCRAT If...

You devote considerable time to
spending taxpayers' money on causes
you support—like gun control.

You Know You're a
REPUBLICAN If...

Now that you're no longer the Republican vice-president, you've got more time for hunting but can't find any willing hunting buddies. So you've settled for taking pot shots at the Democrats—for supporting the Copenhagen global warming summit.

You Know You're a
DEMOCRAT If...

Now that you're no longer the Democratic vice-president, you've finally admitted that you didn't invent the Internet—because you were actually busy inventing the "green movement."

You Know You're a
REPUBLICAN If...

You oppose government subsidized transit, but you expect the public works department to fix that pothole on your street—now!

You Know You're a
DEMOCRAT If...

You support spending billions on taxpayer-subsidized mass transit used by a tiny fraction of the populace while thousands of fellow taxpayers are stuck in traffic jams on overcrowded highways wasting vast amounts of gas.

You Know You're a
REPUBLICAN If...

You thank God every day for the gifts He has bestowed upon you and your family, especially your tax-free inheritance.

You Know You're a
DEMOCRAT If...

You thank God every day for
the strength She gives you
to fight for truth, justice, and
punitive damage awards.

You Know You're a
REPUBLICAN If...

Your dog gets better health
care than your gardener.

You Know You're a
DEMOCRAT If...

You're angry that the new healthcare legislation fell drastically short of providing free, unlimited, universal coverage for basics like maternity care, hearing aids, bone marrow transplants, prosthetics, orthodontics, dental floss, teeth whitening, Botox injections, earwax removal, and, oh yeah, pet care too.

You Know You're a
REPUBLICAN If...

You thought your college professors
were all flaming liberals.

You Know You're a
DEMOCRAT If...

You *are* a college professor.

You Know You're a
REPUBLICAN If...

You think every Democrat
is a closet Communist.

You Know You're a
DEMOCRAT If...

You think every Republican
is closeted.

You Know You're a
REPUBLICAN If...

You equipped your bathroom shower with a wonderful gushing waterfall showerhead, and you don't care if neighbors think you're insensitive about conserving water. You'll pay for all the water you consume as long as they don't increase your taxes to pay for new waterworks.

You Know You're a
DEMOCRAT If...

You only shower twice a week and you've equipped your home with low-volume toilets, a high-efficiency hot water heater, and a "green" clothes dryer. If someone needs to be taxed for new waterworks, make it the other guy. You've already blown a fortune being sensitive.

You Know You're a
REPUBLICAN If...

Your source for illegal
drugs is your maid.

You Know You're a
DEMOCRAT If...

Your source for illegal
drugs is your uncle.

You Know You're a
REPUBLICAN If...

You attend a Tea Party rally because you're frustrated; angry; tired of excessive taxes and wasteful spending; mad at Wall Street; and bitter about health care reform; you don't think Bush was conservative enough; you miss Reagan terribly; you love Palin and hate Obama; and you like to dress up like an eighteenth-century patriot.

You Know You're a
DEMOCRAT If...

You attend a Tea Party rally because
you like to see grown men wear
costumes with funny hats.

You Know You're a
REPUBLICAN If...

You've learned that the secret
to a youthful appearance is
a good personal trainer and
a great plastic surgeon.

You Know You're a
DEMOCRAT If...

You've learned that the secret to a youthful appearance is yoga, soy milk, and a *quiet* plastic surgeon.

You Know You're a
REPUBLICAN If...

You and your third spouse vehemently oppose same-sex marriage as an insult to the sacred institution of matrimony.

You Know You're a
DEMOCRAT If...

You firmly believe that marriage should be allowed between any consenting adults of the same species—although you do know some women who are madly in love with their cats and, well...

You Know You're a
REPUBLICAN If...

You blame your obesity on your hectic schedule and your unrestricted expense account.

You Know You're a
DEMOCRAT If...

You blame your obesity on every fast-food restaurant you've ever visited, your neighborhood grocery store, all the cookie manufacturers, and your mother—and you're gonna sue 'em all!

You Know You're a
REPUBLICAN If...

Now that Obamacare passed,
you think you should be on your
father's "death panel." After all,
you're next in line for the family
fortune, and you want to make
sure he gets appropriate care.

You Know You're a
DEMOCRAT If...

You swear on a stack of Bibles,
Torahs, and Korans that you would
never, ever support death panels
for aged Republicans who have far
too much money. (At least not until
estates are taxed heavily again.)

You Know You're a
REPUBLICAN If...

Your idea of "compassionate conservatism" means giving your employees praise instead of a raise.

You Know You're a
DEMOCRAT If...

Your idea of "liberalism" means
spending other people's money
liberally on causes you support.

You Know You're a
REPUBLICAN If...

You believe human cloning is morally objectionable unless, of course, they figure out how to reincarnate Ronald Reagan.

You Know You're a
DEMOCRAT If...

You think it would be cool
to clone Bill Clinton, maybe
minus a few body parts.

You Know You're a
REPUBLICAN If...

Your car displays a bumper sticker
that says, "The Lord giveth and
the Democrats taketh away."

You Know You're a
DEMOCRAT If...

Your bumper sticker says, "The Lord giveth and the Republicans keepeth. Until now."

You Know You're a
REPUBLICAN If...

You firmly believe in personal privacy in the bedroom, but you draw the line at same-sex couplings.

You Know You're a
DEMOCRAT If...

You firmly believe in personal privacy
in the bedroom, but the thought
of two Republicans procreating
sends shivers down your spine.

You Know You're a
REPUBLICAN If...

You're happy your stockbroker recommended Nike shares fifteen years ago. You try not to think about the fact that your favorite sneakers were manufactured in overseas sweatshops all those years.

You Know You're a
DEMOCRAT If...

You're thrilled that anti-Nike activists
got those overseas sweatshops
shut down. You try not to think
about the thousands of workers
who are now unemployed.

You Know You're a
REPUBLICAN If...

You refused to waste your time reading Internet blogs until you learned that Sean Hannity and Glenn Beck write them. Now you're hooked.

You Know You're a
DEMOCRAT If...

You're pretty sure Al Gore
invented blogs too.

You Know You're a
REPUBLICAN If...

You believe the swine flu scare
was a government-sponsored hoax
perpetrated by the Democrats to
justify foisting federal health care on
everyone, but, just to be sure, you
and your family were first in line at
your private doctor for vaccinations.

You Know You're a
DEMOCRAT If...

You think the swine flu scare was overhyped by Republicans because they own the drug companies that would profit from it, but you made sure your family was first in line for free vaccinations at the county health department.

You Know You're a
REPUBLICAN If...

You're totally baffled by the
Israeli-Palestinian conflict, but
you're certain the Democrats
will mess it up even worse.

You Know You're a
DEMOCRAT If...

You're totally flummoxed by
the Israeli-Palestinian conflict,
but you think the Republicans
really messed it up.

You Know You're a
REPUBLICAN If...

You despise huge federal deficits—unless a Republican president is in office.

You Know You're a
DEMOCRAT If...

You don't like huge deficits either, but your favorite social program sure could use a few hundred billion dollars more.

You Know You're a
REPUBLICAN If...

You own two cows.
Your neighbor has none.
He feels cheated; he wants
one of your cows.
So?

You Know You're a
DEMOCRAT If...

You own two cows.

Your neighbor has none.

He doesn't want a cow; he wants a pig.

You insist that the government give
him a cow; pigs are bad for you.

You still have two cows.

You are happy.

You Know You're a
REPUBLICAN If...

You liked high school.
You studied hard enough to get into
the college you wanted to attend.
You had a girlfriend with nice hair.
Life was good.

You Know You're a
DEMOCRAT If...

You couldn't wait to get
out of high school.
You either were a feminist
or dated one.
You studied your butt off.
You joined the debate team
or the school paper or, better
yet, both. You wore black.

You Know You're a
REPUBLICAN If...

You paid $1,000 to stuff the head of the trophy buck you shot. You share the venison with your business partner.

You Know You're a
DEMOCRAT If...

You paid $1,000 for a guided trout fishing excursion that was, of course, strictly catch-and-release.

You Know You're a
REPUBLICAN If...

You resent paying union dues because
you never like the politicians the
union endorses—even though you
sure like the union pay scale.

You Know You're a
DEMOCRAT If...

You always vote for the candidates your union endorses—as long as they oppose "right-to-work" laws.

You Know You're a
REPUBLICAN If...

You're afraid of the IRS.

You Know You're a
DEMOCRAT If...

You're afraid of the FBI.

You Know You're a
REPUBLICAN If...

You attend a "Save the Wilderness" charity dinner and, while the speaker is rambling on, you daydream about which sauce would taste good on broiled spotted owl.

You Know You're a
DEMOCRAT If...

You refuse to attend the "Save the Wilderness" charity dinner because the chicken being served isn't free range.

You Know You're a
REPUBLICAN If...

Your daughter's coming out
party gets special mention in the
society page of the newspaper.

You Know You're a
DEMOCRAT If...

Your son's coming out party is written
up in the Gay Alliance newsletter.

You Know You're a
REPUBLICAN If...

You feel you must hide your
secret passion for reading
Rolling Stone magazine.

You Know You're a
DEMOCRAT If...

You feel you must hide your secret
passion for watching stock car racing.

You Know You're a
REPUBLICAN If...

You buy a big gas-guzzling SUV, thus sending American dollars to buy oil from Middle East countries where everyone hates America.

You Know You're a
DEMOCRAT If...

You buy a modest Japanese
or German car, thus sending
American dollars and jobs to
European and Asian countries
where everyone hates America.

You Know You're a
REPUBLICAN If...

You don't think all public buildings
need to be wheelchair accessible,
but you believe public lands
should be open to anyone with an
oil rig, an ATV, or a shotgun.

You Know You're a
DEMOCRAT If...

You think every building, including the top of the Washington Monument, should be accessible to those using a wheelchair or Seeing Eye dog, but public lands should be wilderness areas open only to those who can hike five miles in and out.

You Know You're a
REPUBLICAN If...

When you make a racially insensitive remark, you're expected to heap ashes upon your head, throw yourself prostrate on the ground, acknowledge your stupidity, and resign from office.

You Know You're a
DEMOCRAT If...

When you make a racially
insensitive remark, you're
supposed to say, "Oops, sorry."

You Know You're a
REPUBLICAN If...

At your favorite steak house, you like to melt a thick pat of butter on your steak just before devouring it.

You Know You're a
DEMOCRAT If...

You haven't eaten steak or
butter for at least ten years—
at least not in public.

You Know You're a
REPUBLICAN If...

You like the rough and tumble
free market economy–unless
your business needs a massive
government bailout to survive.

You Know You're a
DEMOCRAT If...

You can't stand the thought of government bailouts for huge businesses, unless the union says it's a good idea.

You Know You're a
REPUBLICAN If...

You chuckle that Obama is stuck
with defending the Afghanistan
War, and you drive your Democrat
friends crazy by supporting him.

You Know You're a
DEMOCRAT If...

You just want everyone to get along.

You Know You're a
REPUBLICAN If...

You visited Disney World as a kid, and
the Magic Kingdom castle reminded
you of your family's summer home.

You Know You're a
DEMOCRAT If...

You visited Disney World as a
kid and thought the depiction
of the animatronic bears was
insensitive and speciesist.

You Know You're a
REPUBLICAN If...

You're 100 percent certain that the
one scientist in a thousand who
debunks global warming is right.

You Know You're a
DEMOCRAT If...

You're 100 percent certain that global warming is imminent and you insist that everyone ride the bus (as long as the bus runs on electricity or compressed natural gas or biodiesel or recycled chicken poop).

You Know You're a
REPUBLICAN If...

Hurricane Katrina destroyed your chain of fried chicken restaurants in New Orleans that employed three hundred African Americans, but you're determined to rebuild if the local economy improves.

You Know You're a
DEMOCRAT If...

You're really sad about Katrina but glad there are fewer fried chicken joints, because all that grease is bad for you. Maybe those employees can find nice government jobs working in the unemployment office.

You Know You're a
REPUBLICAN If...

You're a huge fan of government subsidies for wind turbines to generate electricity, as long as you own them.

You Know You're a
DEMOCRAT If...

You're an even bigger fan of
subsidies for wind turbines, as long
as Republicans don't own them.

You Know You're a
REPUBLICAN If...

You consider yourself to be a
seeker of the truth, as long as
it's not *An Inconvenient Truth*.

You Know You're a
DEMOCRAT If...

You seek the truth, and nothing but
the truth, so help you Al Gore.

You Know You're a
REPUBLICAN If...

Your excuse for buying a
gas-guzzling SUV is, "Mind
your own damn business."

You Know You're a
DEMOCRAT If...

Your excuse for buying a gas-guzzling SUV is, "Well, umm, I plan to deliver Meals on Wheels to hungry endangered species in the wilderness."

You Know You're a
REPUBLICAN If...

The phrase "audacity of hope" makes you angry.

You Know You're a
DEMOCRAT If...

The phrase "you betcha" makes
you cringe—or laugh.

You Know You're a
REPUBLICAN If...

Your parents wanted you to go
to college, join the Peace Corps,
and become a teacher. You
joined the NRA and became an
investment banker instead.

You Know You're a
DEMOCRAT If...

Your parents wanted you to go to college, join the Peace Corps, and become a teacher. You did.

You Know You're a
REPUBLICAN If...

You think Glenn Beck and
Rush Limbaugh are intellectual
powerhouses, and you've learned
many insights from their wisdom.

You Know You're a
DEMOCRAT If...

Everything you know about
politics you learned from Jon
Stewart and Stephen Colbert.

You Know You're a
REPUBLICAN If...

You think winning the Nobel Peace
Prize should require doing something.

You Know You're a
DEMOCRAT If...

You danced in the streets and thumbed your nose at Republicans when Obama won the Nobel Peace Prize, even though you don't have the foggiest idea why he got it.

You Know You're a
REPUBLICAN If...

You are appalled that *Harper's Weekly* once referred to a Republican president as a "despot, liar, thief, braggart, buffoon, usurper, monster, old scoundrel, perjurer, swindler, tyrant, field-butcher, land-pirate." Especially since it was Lincoln they were writing about.

You Know You're a
DEMOCRAT If...

Your head still hurts trying to grasp
that Lincoln was a Republican.

You Know You're a
REPUBLICAN If...

You have a good stock portfolio,
but your conscience is nagging
you about your big investment
in tobacco companies.

You Know You're a
DEMOCRAT If...

You have a clear conscience,
but you really miss the days
when smoking was fun.

You Know You're a
REPUBLICAN If...

You wouldn't mind if the
Commonwealth of Massachusetts
seceded from the Union.

You Know You're a
DEMOCRAT If...

You wish the Republic of Texas
had never become a state.

You Know You're a
REPUBLICAN If...

You didn't understand some of the
cynical jokes about Republicans
on the previous pages.

You Know You're a
DEMOCRAT If...

Your feelings were hurt by some of
the mean jokes about Democrats
on the previous pages.

About the Author

Frank Benjamin is the pseudonym of a university vice-president who is (a) cautious, (b) cowardly, (c) modest, (d) all of the above (or perhaps (e) just fond of multiple-choice tests). Now working in the bustling arena of online education, Frank enjoys regular contact with business executives and governors of both political stripes, who, he notes graciously, "usually can laugh at themselves." Usually.